SAYINGS FROM *THE ANALECTS OF CONFUCIUS*

Don't worry when people fail to recognize your merits.
Worry when you fail to recognize theirs.

If you study the past and use it to understand the present,
then you're worthy to be a teacher.

When you meet a worthy person, seek to become his equal.
When you meet a fool, look within and examine yourself.

Always keep in mind the age of your parents.
Let this thought be, on one hand, a source of joy, on the other, of anxiety.

An exemplary person should be slow to speak yet quick to act.

Virtuous people are never lonely. They always attract neighbors.

I wish the old may enjoy peace, friends may enjoy trust,
and the young may enjoy affection.

To truly love something is better than simply to understand it,
and to rejoice in it is better than simply to love it.

To study quietly, to remain always hungry for knowledge,
to teach others without growing weary — all this comes to me naturally.

Even though you have only coarse rice to eat, plain water to drink,
and your bent arm for a pillow, you may still rejoice.
For me, wealth and renown gained without honor are nothing but drifting clouds.

I am fortunate indeed. Whenever I make a mistake, there is always someone to notice it.

Do you want to know what knowledge is?

When you know something, recognize that you know it,

and when you don't know something,

recognize that you don't know it.

That's knowledge.

The Analects of Confucius

Book 2, Chapter 1 7

Arthur A. Levine Books

An Imprint of Scholastic Press

Confucius

THE GOLDEN RULE

BY RUSSELL FREEDMAN

ILLUSTRATED BY FRÉDÉRIC CLÉMENT

Confucius: The Golden Rule

More than 2,500 years have passed since Confucius walked the dusty country roads of China, chatting with his disciples, yet his voice still rings clear and true down through the centuries. Those who knew him never forgot him. Those who came after handed down his sayings from one generation to the next, right up to our own time.

Today, people often think of him as a comic sage, a loony philosopher whose witty remarks always begin, "Confucius say." It's true that he had a sense of humor. He would probably laugh out loud to find that snippets of his "wisdom" are stuffed into fortune cookies, which were invented in America and have never been popular in China.

The real Confucius was a minor government official in the ancient Chinese province of Lu. He lived during troubled times, and he longed to take an active role in running the state. Though he offered many bold ideas for reform, his advice was ignored by the rulers of the day.

For this reason, he spent much of his time teaching and discussing his ideas with his students. So far as realizing his ambitions in his lifetime, he was a failure. But his ideas were so powerful and so full of wisdom that his words are alive after twenty-five centuries, and often, he seems to be speaking directly to us.

A Life of Joy

Tradition tells us that Confucius was a large man possessed of great physical strength. He has been described as a homely giant with warts on his nose, two long front teeth that protruded over his lower lip, and a wispy beard. What people remembered most, however, wasn't his odd appearance but his undeniable charm. Princes confided in him. Wherever he went, loving friends surrounded him.

"What kind of man is he?" asked the governor of a nearby province. He directed his question to Zilu, Confucius's oldest student and closest friend. Zilu wasn't usually at a loss for words, but this time, he didn't know how to reply.

He reported this to Confucius, who said: "Why didn't you just tell him that I'm a man driven by such passion for learning that in my enthusiasm I often forget to eat, in my joy I forget to worry, and I don't even notice the approach of old age." *

Confucius was recognized as one of the most learned men of his day, and he spent many happy hours in libraries, poring over ancient texts. But he was also an energetic man of action, skilled at handling horses, a sure shot with a bow and arrow, a hunter and fisherman, and a bold and tireless traveler who kept setting out on dangerous trips to distant provinces when he was well into his fifties and sixties.

An enthusiast for learning, a man of passion whose sense of joy keeps him always young in spirit — that's how Confucius described himself.

He was no saint, however. Once, a character named Ru Bei sent a messenger to Confucius's home, asking for a meeting. Confucius disapproved of Ru Bei and wanted him to know it. He declined the meeting on the ground that he was ill. Then, as the messenger was going out the door, the wily philosopher took up his lute and began to sing loudly, making sure that he was heard.

---

* All dialogue is from *The Analects of Confucius,* as specified in the endnotes.

He was also an energetic man of action.

Another time, a rude and disrespectful youth incited Confucius to lose his temper. He gave the insolent young man a tongue lashing, then raised his walking stick and cracked the fellow across the shins.

As far as we know, Confucius did not write down his teachings. He shared his ideas with his students through the give and take of informal conversations. After his death, his disciples compiled his sayings in a book called the *Lun Yü*, which means "dialogues" or "conversations" and is usually translated into English as the *Analects*. This slim volume is the one source where we can most clearly hear the unique voice of the real, living Confucius.

Other than that, little is known for certain about the actual events of his life. Yet much has been written about him. Fanciful stories and legends have clustered about his name like iron filings drawn irresistibly to a powerful magnetic field.

At Fifteen, I Set My Heart on Learning

Confucius's family name was Kong. His students knew him as Kongfuzi, or Master Kong. When Jesuit missionaries first visited China in the 16th century, they gave Kongfuzi the Latin name, Confucius, by which he has always been known in the West.

He was born in 551 BC, or thereabouts, in the state of Lu, not far from the modern city of Qufu (chew-foo) in what is now Shandong Province. It is said that his father was a seventy-year-old retired soldier, and his mother a young peasant girl.

Shortly before Confucius was born, according to legend, a unicorn came out of the woods and approached his home. Recognizing the strange and mysterious creature as a good omen, his mother went up to the unicorn and tied a bright ribbon around its horn.

Two days later, she climbed a nearby mountain where she prayed to the mountain spirit for a boy. On her way home, she went into labor and found refuge in a cave, where, the story goes, she gave birth to her baby. He was very ugly, a huge bawling infant with a twisted nose and a strange bulge on his skull. He looked just like his elderly father.

He was given the formal name Kong Qiu (kong chyoh). Records suggest that the Kong clan had been members of the minor nobility centuries earlier, but by the time little Kong Qiu came into the world, the family's fortunes had declined.

He was just three years old when his father died. As we discover in the *Analects*, he grew up in humble circumstances: "We were very poor when I was young," he told his disciples. "That's why I had to learn so many useful skills."

By the time he was a teenager, he knew he had the makings of a scholar. "At fifteen, I set my heart on learning," he said.

Somehow he was able to study, perhaps with a teacher, though he seems to have been largely self-taught. And throughout his life, he never lost his love of books and learning. "Study as if you'll never know enough," he later told his students, "as if you're afraid of losing what you've already gained."

At nineteen, he went to work as manager of a provincial grainery, a responsible job since grain, in those days, was used as money, and his accounts had to be accurate. Then he became supervisor of a wealthy family's grazing lands, where he kept track of oxen and sheep and made sure they were fat and healthy.

During these years, Confucius married. His wife gave birth to a son and a daughter, but we know nothing else about her, not even her name. We don't know how long they were married, if they separated, or if she died. Women did not, as a rule, play a visible role in the public life of ancient China, and while they were influential behind the scenes very often, they are not always mentioned in the historical records. In China as in many other ancient societies, a woman's place was said to be in the home.

Meanwhile, Confucius pursued his studies. Whenever he had a chance, he visited the state capital, Qufu, a lively town thronged with people talking, laughing, and shouting; buying, selling, and gambling; eating at food stalls in every street; and watching acrobats, jugglers, and magicians at the marketplace, where vendors hawked such delicacies as bears' paws, the fins of sharks, the livers of peacocks, and bees fried in their own honey.

In Qufu, he could find books of history and literature that weren't available at the country estates where he worked. He studied texts that reached far back in time, among them the *Shujing* or *Book of History*, which recounted the words and deeds of the the old hero-kings, and the *Shijing* or *Book of Songs*, a collection of ancient folk songs, poems, and hymns. Books back then were bulky and clumsy. Copies were few. They were inscribed with a stylus on strips of bamboo

A lively town thronged with people

bound together by leather cords, resembling Venetian blinds. Paper, a Chinese invention, would not appear for another six hundred years.

It seems that Confucius didn't want to spend his life keeping tabs on herds of livestock and sacks of grain. He was ambitious and hoped for a chance at serious government work, yet he wasn't offered the kind of position he wanted. Perhaps he was too outspoken. As he studied China's glorious past and its turbulent present, he developed radical ideas about good government. And he didn't hesitate to criticize the proud feudal lords who ruled the state of Lu.

Since he lacked an official position, he talked about his ideas with friends and acquaintances. He must have been very persuasive, for he attracted a growing number of young men who became his students. At first, most of them were men his own age or a little younger. Like Confucius, they hoped to become government officials so they could introduce reforms that would help bring peace to China's embattled states and justice to its downtrodden people.

Dangerous Ideas

China was a land in crisis. Centuries earlier, the Middle Kingdom, as China was known, had been peaceful and unified under the kings of the Zhou Dynasty. Since then, the central government had lost all control. A Zhou king still sat on the imperial throne, but now he was nothing more than a weak and useless figurehead.

Real power lay in the hands of the feudal lords, rich landowners with private armies who fought constantly among themselves. China had splintered into an unruly collection of small, independent, warring states. Even the greatest noble could not feel secure, for he knew he could be ruined or even assassinated at any time. But the common people were the ones who suffered most. The aristocrats taxed the people severely to pay for their private armies and support their lavish style of living, and they suppressed all protests ruthlessly. When harvests were poor, thousands of peasants starved.

Confucius believed that he was witnessing the collapse of China's ancient civilization. He looked back to that distant Golden Age under the early Zhou kings, when the rulers were men of virtue and ordinary people went out of their way to act decently. And he searched for ways to stop the anarchy and decline he saw all around him.

Voting was unknown in ancient China. The warring states were governed by men who had inherited their rank in society and their posts as government ministers. Many of these nobles lacked the skill and interest to perform their duties. They treated their offices as part of their birthright, used their privileges to enrich themselves, and led extravagant lives.

"You can't expect anything from men who stuff themselves with food all day

China had splintered into an unruly collection of small, independent, warring states.

and never use their minds," Confucius complained. "Even gamblers do something, which is surely better than doing nothing at all."

He asked himself: *What is the purpose of government? It is to promote the welfare and happiness of the people — all the people*, he decided. An incompetent ruler or corrupt official forfeits the people's trust, and when trust is lost, the country is doomed. Confucius told his students that it was their duty to criticize any ruler who abused his power — even at the risk of their lives.

This was a dangerous idea in an age when a displeased prince, with a wave of his hand, could order that a man be boiled alive. And yet Confucius had the nerve to go even further. The right to govern, he declared, should depend on a person's character and ability, not on his birth. If a government is to succeed, it must be administered by the most capable people in the country.

Confucius did not ask that the rulers of his day give up their inherited thrones — that would have been going too far and might have resulted in the loss of his head. Instead, he suggested that those in power might continue to reign but not actually govern, delegating real authority to ministers chosen solely for their ability.

There was just one way that those ministers could acquire the skill and knowledge they would need to govern wisely: through education. Until then, education had been regarded as useful only for the sons of noble families. Confucius insisted that education be open to all, rich or poor, nobleman or commoner, so that every young man of ability, no matter how humble, might have a chance to serve as a leader. "When people are educated, distinctions between classes disappear," he said.

Acting on his beliefs, he took his students from every background, welcoming barefoot peasant boys into his circle along with the sons of princes, hoping to shape them into statesmen. His revolutionary stand would earn him a saint's reputation among future generations of Chinese teachers. "I never denied my teaching to anyone who sought it," he said, "even if he came to me on foot with nothing more to offer as tuition than a package of dried meat."

He had just one requirement: A student had to demonstrate a passion for learning. "I teach only those who burst with enthusiasm. I guide only those who are struggling to learn themselves. If I explain one corner of a subject, I expect the student to discover the other three for himself, and if he doesn't, I don't continue the lesson."

Confucius's favorite student was the shy and quiet Yan Hui, who was younger than Confucius by some thirty years. He came from a poor family and knew how it felt to be hungry, which simply added to Confucius's admiration for him. Yan Hui endeared himself to the Master by his eagerness to learn and his sincerity, yet he was extremely modest. He spoke so softly, when he spoke at all, that everyone had to lean forward, ears cupped, to catch what he was saying.

Like so many of history's great teachers, Confucius understood that the beginning of wisdom is to recognize the limits of your knowledge. "Do you want to know what knowledge is?" he asked. "When you know something, recognize that you know it, and when you don't know something, recognize that you don't know it. That's knowledge."

He trained his students in the ancient rites and ceremonies that every government official was expected to know. But more important, he prodded them to think in new ways. "If a person learns from others but doesn't think, he will be bewildered," he said. "But to think without learning — that's really dangerous."

We can picture him in the capital city of Qufu, sitting on a terrace in the shade of an apricot tree, or in a cool tiled pavilion, engaged in spirited discussions with his students. He invited them to disagree with him and sometimes said frankly that they were right and he was wrong.

He had a keen appreciation of each student's individual character. When Zilu

We can picture him sitting on a terrace in the shade of an apricot tree.

Confucius set out on his long and perilous travels to distant provinces.

asked, "Shall I practice at once what I have just learned?" Confucius is said to have replied, "No! Don't do it before you have talked it over with your father and your elder brother." But when Ranyou wanted to try out the same idea, Confucius said, "Go ahead! Do it at once!"

A student who had heard both conversations was puzzled. Confucius explained: "Ranyou takes forever to start anything, so I try to urge him on. Zilu is too impulsive, so I hold him back."

Confucius was finally given a responsible post when a new ruler in Lu, Duke Ding, appointed him governor of a small district. Apparently he did so well as governor that he was made police commissioner of Lu, and in this post, tradition says, he ensured peace and order throughout the province. We are told that objects lost by their owners were always returned, doors were left unlocked without fear of burglary, the sellers of lambs and suckling pigs did not adulterate their meat, and men and women walked on opposite sides of the street, as was considered right and proper.

But it seems that Duke Ding didn't live up to Confucius's idea of what a moral leader should be, and around 497 BC, when he was fifty-four years old, Confucius quit his post and with some of his students set out on his long and perilous travels to distant provinces.

Travels in the Middle Kingdom

Confucius was searching for an enlightened ruler who would allow him to put his ideas about government into practice. He never found one. At each stop, he was received with courtesy and respect, at least at first. Dukes and princes invited him into their courts as an honored sage and questioned him about his ideas. But none of them were willing to put real power into his hands.

His views must have seemed threatening. Corrupt ministers who had inherited their offices feared that if Confucius and his disciples ever gained a foothold at court, they themselves soon would be without employment. Dukes and princes knew they would have a hard time meeting the Master Kong's strict standards.

Confucius refused to flatter the high and mighty, and he did not mince words. Once, when a powerful noble asked how he might deal effectively with thieves, the philosopher told him: "If you yourself, Sir, were not on the take, no one would be trying to steal from you."

At times, his political enemies, suspecting that he might gain influence, conspired against him. They whispered that he couldn't be trusted, that he was a spy in the pay of the state of Lu. Once, we are told, while he was traveling through the state of Song, soldiers loyal to a local lord plotted to waylay and assassinate him at a dusty country crossroads. The plan was discovered, and Confucius escaped unharmed. After that, he traveled in disguise, driving his own chariot through fortified towns, past burned-out castles and looted temples, moving across a countryside haunted by ghosts, strewn with the giant bones of creatures said to be dragons, and terrorized by marauding rebels and bandits.

One day, he was mistaken for one of those bandits. As he arrived in a strange

Moving across a countryside haunted by ghosts...

town and climbed out of his chariot, the townsfolk took one look at the towering bearded sage and concluded that he must be that other well-known giant — the notorious Yan Huo, who rode up and down the land sacking and plundering. Confucius and his companions were seized and dragged off to prison. They remained locked up for five days before the townspeople finally admitted that they had the wrong man.

In the midst of all this confusion, Confucius's beloved student, the gentle and soft-spoken Yan Hui, became separated from the rest of the group. Confucius worried about him, and when they reunited he was greatly relieved. "I thought you were dead," he told Yan Hui.

"While you, Master, are alive, how would I dare to die?" was Yan Hui's famous reply.

Wherever he went, Confucius seemed to fit in and feel right at home. "How does he manage to learn so much about the places he visits?" his student Zigong was asked. "Does he ask for such information, or is it given him?"

"He gets it by being cordial, good-natured, courteous, deferential — that's how he learns so much," Zigong replied. "The Master has a way of inquiring that is quite different from other people's, don't you think?"

Confucius himself said that he acquired information by using his eyes and ears: "I listen carefully, pick out what is best, and follow it myself. I see many things, and I remember them."

Whenever he had a chance, he went out to a field to practice his archery. He was fond of fishing, and he would sit quietly on a riverbank with a bamboo pole, a silken line, a bronze hook, and a wicker basket for his catch. He loved music and he made friends with the blind court musicians he met, listened to their playing, and joined in their songs and chants. It is said that he knew the ancient *Book of Songs* so well, he could sing every one of those 305 songs from memory.

"I see many things, and I remember them."

ADA COMMUNITY LIBRARY

"I'd like to go wandering with a bunch of friends."

He was chatting with some of his disciples one day when he asked: "Now tell me honestly — given the opportunity, what would you most want to do?"

Zilu rushed to reply first: "Put me in charge of a small country squeezed between powerful neighbors and threatened by invading armies, and I'll bring courage and direction to the people."

Confucius smiled. "And what about you, Ranyou?" he asked.

"Give me a country in the grip of a famine, and I'll secure the people's prosperity in no time at all!"

"Zihua, how about you?"

"I'd like to put on the ceremonial cap and robes of an important official and take part in a diplomatic conference."

Zengxi was the last to speak. He had been playing his lute softly as he listened to the others. Plucking one last chord, he pushed the instrument aside and said: "I'm afraid my wish isn't up to those of my three companions."

"There's no harm in that," Confucius replied. "After all, each of us is simply confiding his personal ambition."

"Well, then," said Zengxi, "on a nice spring day, after all the spring clothes have been made, I'd like to go wandering with a bunch of friends, have a swim in the Yi River, enjoy the breeze on the Rain Dance Terrace, then wander back home singing."

Confucius heaved a deep sigh. "I'm with you, Zengxi," he said, "I'm with you."

The Golden Rule

Zilu asked Confucius: "If you could take over a government, what's the first thing you would do?"

"I would start using honest language. Without a doubt, I'd want to call things by their right names."

"Are you kidding?" replied Zilu, who loved to argue with Confucius. "What does language have to do with governing?"

"Listen, Zilu. If we don't call things by their correct names, then words don't mean a thing. When words don't match reality, what is said isn't the same as what is meant. And when what is said isn't the same as what is meant, we can't think clearly and nothing can be accomplished. Calling things by their right names makes it possible for us to speak truthfully about them."

In Confucius's day (as in ours), many things were not called by their right names. China considered itself the Middle Kingdom, but it was less a kingdom than a rabble of warring states. Men who called themselves noble princes were in truth cruel tyrants. Government ministers were thieves and assassins. Justice was a word lost in the turmoil of the times.

The first task of a true statesman, Confucius said, is to face the truth, to use words honestly, and that's what he himself endeavored to do. If a prince wanted to be called a prince, then he had to act like one.

Confucius took aim at one word, in particular. Up to his time, the Chinese term *junzi* (君子), or "gentleman," meant literally a "lord's son," someone who occupied a position of power and prestige because of birth. Without the right ancestors, no man could hope to become a gentleman. And no gentleman could ever become less than one, no matter how badly he behaved.

26

The first task of a true statesman, Confucius said, is to face the truth.

That's nonsense, Confucius declared. He insisted that a true gentleman is made, not born. A man's worth depends on what he is, not on what his grandfather was. Just having the right ancestors isn't enough. Being a *junzi*, said Confucius, is a matter of noble conduct and character, not noble birth.

This was another of his revolutionary ideas. He took the exclusive right to be called a gentleman away from a few ruling families and gave that honor to anyone who earned it. And if a commoner could earn the right to be called a gentleman, then the chance to serve as a leader, to hold a position of power and influence, was open to all.

While *junzi* is usually translated as "gentleman," reflecting the patriarchal world of ancient China, the term does not necessarily carry a masculine meaning. *Junzi* can also be interpreted to mean an "exemplary person" of any gender. Scholars of classical Chinese have pointed out that when the *Analects* were being compiled, women could be regarded as having some of the same noble qualities that Confucius assigned to the *junzi*. Confucius himself singled out a woman known as Ji of Lu, praising her expert knowledge of the sacred rites. And at least one of the ancient hero-kings, King Wu, had counted a woman among the ten ministers of his governing council.

A true *junzi*, said Confucius, is someone who works hard to master the art of government and the rules of virtuous behavior. "An exemplary person," he said, "helps bring out what is beautiful in other people and discourages what is ugly in them. A petty person does just the opposite."

Above all, an exemplary person must endeavor to practice what the Chinese call *ren* (仁), which can be understood as "a compassionate love for humanity." *Ren* is hard to translate because it is an all-embracing term that combines qualities like kindness, benevolence, and virtue; it means treating people decently, beginning with the members of one's own family. For it is in the family that an individual learns respect and cooperation and gains experience dealing with others.

Confucius placed great emphasis on family obligations. He said many times that

"An exemplary person," he said, "helps bring out what is beautiful in other people and discourages what is ugly in them. A petty person does just the opposite."

young people should honor their parents and respect their elders. But he also said that the young are entitled to the same consideration, for a hard-hearted father is just as bad as a disrespectful son: "Young people should not be taken lightly. How do you know that they will not one day be better than you are now?"

The secret of a successful society is harmony, he taught. And the way to achieve harmony in human affairs is to observe those manners and customs that express a society's shared values and traditions and help bind the society together — what the Chinese call *li* (利). The great public rituals of temple and state, such as religious ceremonies, and the small intimate rites of personal life, such as etiquette and simple courtesy, are equally important as the cement of society.

"Wherever you go in the world," Confucius told his students, "you should treat all those whom you meet as if you are receiving a highly honored guest."

Confucianism has been called a religion, but Confucius the man was not a religious prophet or teacher. While he approved of those religious ceremonies that honored the ancestors and reminded people of their unity with all those who came before, he was reluctant to discuss such matters as the meaning of life and death or the destiny of the soul.

"May I ask you about death?" Zilu is said to have asked. And Confucius replied: "If we do not yet understand life, how can we understand death?"

The world that mattered to Confucius was this world, the living world. He talked about the here and now, about the ethical path that we should follow here on earth, what he called the Way.

"Is there any single word that could guide a person's entire life?" asked his student Zigong.

"Perhaps it is *shu* (恕)," Confucius replied, using a word that means "compassion," "open-heartedness," or "caring for others." Then he went on to explain: "Do not impose on others what you do not wish for yourself."

Five centuries later, Jesus taught the Golden Rule with similar words: "In everything, do to others as you would have them do to you."

The Unicorn Returns

Confucius wandered through the warring states of ancient China for perhaps thirteen years, searching in vain for a ruler who would give him a chance to test his ideas. Once, as his procession arrived at a city gate, a sentry asked, "Who is that old man?"

"That's the great sage, the Master Kong," a disciple replied.

"Ah, yes," the sentry laughed. "He's the one who is always saying that even though it's no use, you have to keep trying."

In 484 BC, when he was sixty-seven, Confucius finally returned to his home state, Lu. He no longer entertained visions of becoming a government official, so he settled down in his house in Qufu and devoted the rest of his life to dialogues with his growing company of students, and to his own studies of history, music, and literature.

His final years were saddened by the deaths of two disciples. His only son, Kong Li, who had spent his life in his father's shadow, died soon after Confucius returned from his travels. Two years later, the philosopher's cherished student Yan Hui — who had said that he dared not die while his master was alive — passed away at the age of thirty-two. Confucius had looked upon Yan Hui as his successor, who would carry on his teachings after he was gone. When the younger man died prematurely, the old philosopher was devastated.

His wild grief alarmed everyone around him. Dressed in mourning, he sat on a plain mat in a room filled with disciples who could not console him. He wailed and wept. "Alas! Heaven is destroying me!" he cried. "Heaven is destroying me!"

"Master, you have abandoned all restraint," Zilu told him. "Such wailing is unseemly. You are showing excessive grief."

It still had a tattered bit of ribbon around its horn.

"Am I? If not for him, then for whom should I show excessive grief?" And Confucius wept fresh tears.

At about this time, according to legend, a strange animal was killed in Lu. Since no one knew what the creature was, it was placed in a wagon and taken to Confucius, who took one look and identified it as a unicorn. It still had a tattered bit of ribbon around its horn that Confucius's mother had tied there seventy years before.

To wound a Chinese unicorn, or to come across its dead body, was known to be a bad omen. Now Confucius wept anew, because he felt what the death of that innocent creature foretold, and because in that shred of ribbon, he saw his own past.

Not long afterwards, he fell ill and lapsed into unconsciousness. Thinking that the Master was dying, Zilu had several disciples dress up in formal court robes, as though they were important ministers of state. They stood by the philosopher's bedside like the retainers he would have had if he had realized his ambition to be a high official, and they began to sway and moan.

Confucius opened his eyes. He looked startled. In a surprisingly strong voice, he said, "Zilu! What on earth do you think you are doing? This is a farce, and it has lasted long enough! When you pretend that I'm something I'm not, whom do you fool? Can I fool the court? Can I deceive heaven? Isn't it better that I should die in the arms of you, my friends, than among false retainers?"

He did not die, not then. He recovered from that illness and returned to his teaching and his studies. Young men came from far and wide to sit at his feet and be warmed by his wisdom and wit. He had failed to win the trust of the rulers he approached, and yet he seemed content:

"Isn't it a pleasure to study and practice what one learns? Isn't it a joy to greet friends who come from afar? Isn't it the mark of a gentleman to bear no resentment when your merits are ignored?"

One morning in the year 479 BC, when he was seventy-two, Confucius woke early, tradition tells us, walked about the courtyard, then announced: "I wish to speak no more." Then he returned to his bedroom, lay on his couch, and stayed there, day after day.

A crowd of silent, watchful young men gathered in the street in front of his house. The disciples, dressed this time in proper mourning, waited in an outer room. The sweet odor of aromatic leaves, burning in the philosopher's bedroom to drive off evil spirits, filled the house.

On the seventh day, Confucius was dead. His disciples buried him on the river bank just north of Qufu, in a grave that has since been visited by countless emperors, officials, and ordinary citizens, and is still attracting visitors today.

The Spirit of Confucius

After Confucius's death, his disciples scattered and traveled throughout China as teachers, government ministers, and court advisers. They spread the doctrine that those who govern should be chosen not for their birth, but for their virtue and ability, and that the true goal of government is the welfare and happiness of all the people.

An influential Confucian scholar known as Mencius, who flourished 150 years after Confucius, carried the Master's ideas a step further. He declared that a ruler must have the consent of the people before he can govern effectively. "If the king fails and oppresses the people," he wrote, "then the people have the right to dispose of him. . . . The common people are the most important element in the state. The sovereign is the least." A king who behaves like a tyrant is a king no more, said Mencius — echoing the Confucian command to call things by their right names.

Confucius had urged his followers to defend their principles even at the cost of their lives, and eventually, that's exactly what happened. In 221 BC, a victorious band of warlords seized power in China and united the warring feudal states under the First August Emperor of the Qin (cheen), founder of the Chinese empire. His dynasty, the Qin, gave China its name! During his brief reign, the young emperor established a strict military state, standardized the writing system, built the Great Wall, and launched a campaign of terror against the dangerous ideas of Mencius and Confucius. Hundreds of Confucian scholars and teachers were rounded up and put to death for daring to criticize the First Emperor of Qin. Their books were burned, their teachings forbidden. Those scholars who escaped fled to the hills and went into hiding.

The emperor ordered his soldiers to break into the philosopher's tomb.

That much is accepted historical fact. According to a popular legend, the emperor was so determined to wipe out every trace of Confucius's influence, he ordered his soldiers to break into the philosopher's tomb. They discovered an underground chamber furnished with a bed and a table, but Confucius was nowhere to be found. A note had been left on the table. The emperor sat down to read it.

"You have broken into my grave," it said, "you are sitting on my bed, and you are reading my note." Just then, the emperor was startled by a rustling sound. A rabbit scurried out of the chamber and ran into the woods. Convinced that the rabbit was the spirit of Confucius, the emperor shouted to the soldiers to chase the little animal and kill it, but it escaped. As the emperor stood at the edge of the woods, furious, he felt a gust of wind, then a chill. The next day he came down with a fever and died.

That's the legend. We know for a fact that the First Emperor of Qin did die in 210 BC and was succeeded by a weakling son. The brutal Qin Dynasty lasted just fifteen years before it was overthrown by a rebellion in which the surviving Confucian scholars played a prominent role.

A century later, Confucius's grave was visited by the great Chinese historian, Sima Qian (sz-ma chyen). "Filled with veneration, I lingered and could hardly tear myself away," he wrote. "On earth there have been many princes and sages, famous during their lifetime, but all was over with them at their death. Confucius was a simple man of the people. But his teachings have been handed down for ten generations."

During the generations that followed, the teachings of Confucius inspired sweeping political reforms. His insistence that government jobs be given to those who are best qualified led to a landmark Chinese invention: the civil service exam, a long written test, open to all, designed to recruit the most knowledgeable people for public service. These competitive exams made it possible for bright young Chinese from poor rural backgrounds to join the ranks of government officials.

In time, Confucian ideals spread to Japan, Korea, and Vietnam. It has been suggested that the Asian emphasis on education reflects the continuing influence of Confucius.

Meanwhile, many of the philosopher's original ideas were being buried under a growing mountain of commentary and interpretation. Competing schools of thought bent the Master's teachings to suit their own purposes, often misrepresenting what he had to say. He was credited with books he didn't write and words he didn't speak, depicting an authoritarian Confucius very different from the questioning teacher found in the *Analects*. It is doubtful that the real Confucius would recognize the elaborate doctrine that later generations called Confucianism.

And while Confucianism is more a philosophy than a religion, lacking the monks and nuns found in other world religions, it has inspired the creation of temples and shrines throughout China, where pilgrims, scholars, and even the emperor himself could offer reverence to the spirit of the great sage, and where Confucius and his original disciples are still being worshipped.

The most famous Confucian temple, a spacious expanse of red tile roofs and ancient, twisted pines and cypresses, stands in the center of Qufu, his hometown. First built in 478 BC as a simple memorial, it has been enlarged, remodeled, added-to, and rebuilt many times over the centuries. It is the site of a colorful ceremony held on September 28 every year, when visitors from all over the world visit Qufu to help celebrate the anniversary of the philosopher's birth.

In the Western world, Confucius's influence has been far greater than many people realize. He was introduced to Western readers by the Jesuit missionaries who traveled to Asia in the 16th century and later became scholars and even officials at the Chinese court. They began to translate the great books of the Orient into Latin, and it was then that the *Lun Yü*, the collected discourses of the sage Kongfuzi, first became known in Europe as *The Analects of Confucius*.

A large number of European philosophers, statesmen, and writers discovered, to their astonishment, that more than 2,000 years earlier, in the "mysterious

The most famous Confucian temple, a spacious expanse of red tile roofs
and ancient, twisted pines and cypresses, stands in the center of Qufu.

Orient," a Chinese sage had been thinking some of the same thoughts they were thinking. They were impressed by Confucius's teachings about the honest use of language, by his attacks on hereditary privilege, and by his ideas concerning good government. They took special note of the doctrine that a ruler must have the consent of his people, and if he fails in his duties, then the people have the moral right of revolution.

These ideas were in the air. They influenced the development of democratic ideals both in Europe and America, and found expression in Thomas Jefferson's preamble to the Declaration of Independence:

"Governments are instituted among men, deriving their just powers from the consent of the governed. . . . Whenever any form of government becomes destructive of these ends, it is the right of the people to alter or to abolish it, and to institute a new government."

In Asia today, those in power still call upon Confucius, hoping to show that he would have favored their views. The leaders of authoritarian regimes seek to justify their rule by emphasizing those teachings that prescribe respect for authority, while ignoring Confucius's beliefs about social justice and political dissent. The leaders of democratic societies in Asia find their inspiration in Confucian ideals of human dignity, individual worth, and the rights of the people against despotism.

And so, after twenty-five centuries, the pros and cons of what Confucius said or didn't say are still being debated. The reason isn't hard to find. He trusted people to think for themselves. He was always ready to offer suggestions, but he insisted that each of us must find answers for ourselves. And he admitted that he himself did not know the truth, only a way to look for it.

"If a person doesn't constantly ask himself, 'What is the right thing to do?' I really don't know what is to be done about him."

So said Confucius.

In Asia today, those in power still call upon Confucius.

Author's Note

In September of the year 2000, my pursuit of Confucius led me and a Mandarin-speaking friend to the Chinese city of Qufu in Shandong Province, formerly the independent state of Lu, where Confucius was born, spent much of his life, and died. Ages ago, Qufu was the capital city of Lu. Today it is a flourishing country town dotted with temples, museums, and shrines dedicated to a favorite son who lived here twenty-five centuries ago.

Every year on September 28, Qufu celebrates the birth of Confucius. My friend and I attended the ceremony commemorating the philosopher's 2551st birthday, a festive event held on the sprawling grounds of the Confucian Temple that dominates the center of Qufu. Hundreds of marchers, dancers, and musicians, wearing traditional silk robes in brilliant hues of vermilion, turquoise, and royal blue, carrying feathered banners and plumes, playing horns and lutes, cymbals, drums, and bells, paraded through the temple grounds and around a lacquer-red shrine as a resplendently attired speaker stood beneath the Gate of Esteeming the Lofty and read selections from the *Analects* — the sayings of Confucius.

Delegates from Confucian societies all over the world were there, along with Chinese government officials and dozens of the philosopher's direct descendants, members of the 77th, 78th, and 79th generations. We looked on as each honored guest approached the shrine in turn and bowed deeply, paying respects to the spirit of the sage as drums rattled and cymbals clanged.

Among the descendants were two half-British schoolchildren, twelve-year-old (Sophie) Kong Chui Yan, dressed in a pink embroidered silk robe, and her small brother, seven-year-old (James) Kong Chui Xu, squirming and shy in gold silk. The middle name Chui instantly identifies them as 79th-generation descendants, according to strict rules laid down by an 18th-century emperor. Sophie and James live in London. They had traveled to Qufu with their parents — their mother is British, their father Chinese — to take part in the ceremonies and make offerings at the family tombs. Earlier, we were told, they had bowed with their elders in front of a freshly killed cow, pig, and sheep, to the mournful tooting of long brass horns. Watching these Eurasian youngsters as they observed solemn ancient rites, I was reminded of the Confucian saying, "All within the Four Seas are brothers."

A popular legend says that Confucius was born some fifteen miles to the south of Qufu, in a cave at the foot of Nishan Mountain, where his mother had taken refuge after suddenly going into labor. We wanted to see that cave for ourselves, so with a guide we drove out of town past rice fields, apple orchards, and mud-walled villages to the mountain. A gravel footpath led us down a rocky hillside to a wooden bridge that crossed a small creek. There we saw the entrance to the cave, marked by a stone tablet that says simply: "Cave of Confucius." We peered inside. It seemed a very small cave indeed, a cramped, dark, and damp place for such an epochal figure to come into the world.

While the actual site and date of Confucius's birth are uncertain, there appears to be little question about the location of the philosopher's grave. He lies buried just north of Qufu in the Confucian Forest, along with thousands of his direct and indirect descendants. Scattered through this lush and haunting forest — considered the largest family cemetery in the world — are dozens of temples and pavilions and hundreds of sculptures, tablets, and tombstones. The grave of the Great Sage himself, however, is disarmingly simple: a grass-covered mound enclosed by a low wall and marked by a dignified Ming Dynasty stele. His son and grandson are buried nearby.

Back in the center of Qufu, we paused at the town's busy main intersection, waiting to cross the street against a noisy stream of automobiles, trucks, and pedi-cabs. Overhead, a huge banner was stretched above the intersection. It displayed yet another saying from the *Analects*:有朋自遠方來，不亦樂乎?, which means, "Isn't it a joy to greet friends who come from afar?"

Russell Freedman, New York City, September 1, 2001

IN SEARCH OF CONFUCIUS: A NOTE ON SOURCES AND SUGGESTIONS FOR FURTHER READING

Confucius does not seem to have written anything that is conclusively attributable to him. Like other great teachers of the ancient world — Socrates, Buddha, Jesus — he taught by means of dialogue and example.

After he died, his disciples began to set down briefly what they remembered of their conversations with him. This process was continued by disciples of the original disciples, and then by other followers for several generations, with the result that the volume we now know as the *Analects* — the "sayings of Confucius" — was perhaps three centuries in the making. While parts of the *Analects* are of doubtful authenticity, the book in general offers the purest record we have of the Master Kong's actual words. It is the one place where we can encounter the real, living Confucius.

Scholars seeking to reconstruct the events of Confucius's life rely first on what they can glean from the *Analects*, and then on records written down as near as possible to his own time. Since works written after the Master had been dead for centuries give much more detailed information about him than those written closer to his lifetime, it is assumed that much of the added information was inspired more by imagination than by any actual events of Confucius's life.

The book known as the *Mencius*, after the philosopher of that name, is considered a valuable source. Written perhaps a century and a half after Confucius's death, it records traditions about him in some detail and in a form similar to that found in the early parts of the *Analects*. The *Zuo Commentary to the Spring and Autumn Annals*, written in its present form nearly two centuries after Confucius, records in much detail the history of the philosopher's native state during the period of his lifetime but tells us little about the life of the sage himself. The standard source for the events of Confucius's life has always been the biography that appears as chapter 47 of the *Records of the Historian*, written about 100 B.C. by Sima Qian. By then, so much legend had accumulated around the figure of the sage that the events it records are considered unreliable if not confirmed by earlier sources.

For today's reader, the most direct, accessible, and enjoyable introduction to the quirky and passionate man we remember as Confucius is to dip into a good edition of the *Analects*. There are many English translations of the *Analects*, and they are all different. Because of the difficulties in interpreting classical Chinese, each translation has its own character and style. For my account of Confucius's life and teachings, I found the following translations, all available as paperbacks, especially helpful:

The Analects of Confucius, translation and annotated by Simon Leys (New York: W.W. Norton and Company, 1997). One of the most persuasive recent translations, accompanied by extensive commentary and notes.

The Analects of Confucius: A Philosophical Translation, by Roger T. Ames and Henry Rosemont, Jr. (New York: Ballantine Books, 1998). A translation based on the earliest version of the *Analects* discovered so far, a partial text dating back to 55 B.C. and made available to scholars in 1997. Includes both Chinese and English texts.

The Analects: Confucius, translated by David Hinton (Washington, D.C.: Counterpoint, 1998). By the award-winning translator of several Chinese poets and philosophers.

Confucius: The Analects, translated with an introduction by D.C. Lau (New York: Penguin Books, 1979). Includes appendices on events in the life of Confucius, on the *Analects* themselves, and on the disciples as they appear in the *Analects*.

The Analects of Confucius, translated and annotated by Arthur Waley

(New York: Vintage Books, 1989; originally published by the Macmillan Company, New York, in 1938). A classic translation by a noted authority.

The above editions of the *Analects* all include informative accounts of Confucius's life. For an authoritative full-length biography, see *Confucius and the Chinese Way*, by H.G. Creel (New York: Harper Torchbooks, 1960; originally published by the John Day Company in 1949 under the title *Confucius: The Man and the Myth*). Creel is also the author of *Chinese Thought: From Confucius to Mao Tse-Tung* (Chicago: The University of Chicago Press, 1953). Another useful survey is *A Short History of Chinese Philosophy: A Systematic Account of Chinese Thought From Its Origins to the Present Day*, by Fung Yu-lan, edited by Derk Bodde (New York: The Free Press, 1997; originally published by Macmillan in 1948).

Sharing the Light: Representations of Women and Virtue in Early China, by Lisa Raphals (Albany: State University of New York Press, 1998), is a scholarly exploration of narratives depicting the lives of women in ancient China. A professor of Asian Studies at Bard College, Raphals challenges certain traditional characterizations concerning the role and influence of women in early China.

Confucius Lives Next Door: What Living in the East Teaches Us About Living in the West, by T.R. Reid (New York: Vintage Books, 2000), offers a provocative discussion of the impact of Confucian ideals on the contemporary world. The book includes, in one chapter, a lively portrayal of Confucius the man.

A unique book suitable for younger readers (or for anyone) presents the wisdom of Confucius in engaging comic-strip form, with a text in both Chinese and English: *Confucius Speaks: Words to Live By*, adapted and illustrated by the cartoonist Tsai Chih Chung, translated by Brian Bruys (New York: Anchor Books, 1996). *Confucius: In Life and Legend*, by Betty Kelen (Singapore: Graham Brash Ltd., 1983; first published in the United States by Thomas Nelson in 1971), is a more conventional biography intended for younger readers.

Finally, Confucius holds forth today on the Internet. Numerous Web sites in many languages are dedicated to the Chinese sage. He can be accessed by typing in "Confucius," "Kong Fuzi," or "Kung Fu-tzu" on any Internet search engine.

SOURCES OF QUOTATIONS
FROM *THE ANALECTS OF CONFUCIUS*

Numerical references follow the traditional nomenclature as used by Ames and Rosemont, e.g.: Book 7. Chapter 19. It should be noted that English translations of the *Analects* differ significantly. The translations offered here are drawn from the five editions of the *Analects* cited in the bibliography and from contemporary Chinese versions translated for me by Patrick Wing-kin Chan, Ivan Chi-lap Ng, and Evans Chan.

To Chan Yiu Shing — R.F.

LIBRARY OF CONGRESS CATALOGING-IN-PUBLICATION DATA

FREEDMAN, RUSSELL.

CONFUCIUS / BY RUSSELL FREEDMAN, ILLUSTRATED BY FRÉDÉRIC CLÉMENT.

P. CM.

ISBN 0-439-13957-0

1. CONFUCIUS — JUVENILE LITERATURE. [1. CONFUCIUS. 2. PHILOSOPHERS.] I. CLÉMENT, FRÉDÉRIC, ILL. II. TITLE.

B128.C8 F73 2002 • 181'.112 — DC21 [B] • 2001029372

10 9 8 7 6 5 4 3 2 1   02 03 04 05 06

BOOK DESIGN BY ELIZABETH B. PARISI • PRINTED IN SINGAPORE ON ACID-FREE PAPER 46
FIRST EDITION, SEPTEMBER 2002

Above all, be loyal to others and trustworthy in what you say.
Befriend only those who are kindred spirits.
And when you are wrong, don't be afraid to change.

A powerful army can be robbed of its commander-in-chief,
but even the humblest people cannot be robbed of their free will.

Don't try to rush things,
and don't think about small gains.
If you are impatient, you may never reach your goal.
If you pursue petty gains, you'll never achieve great things.

A humane person is always courageous,
but a courageous person is not necessarily humane.

A promise easily made is hard to keep.

In any matter, if you don't think far into the future,
trouble will be close at hand.

Demand much from yourself, little from others,
and you will avoid resentment.

In the pursuit of virtue, don't be afraid to overtake your teacher.

Human beings are similar by nature.
It's the experience of living that makes us so different.

Clever talk and affected manners are seldom signs of goodness.